ASIAPAC COMI

LIVING 21 SE

The Chinese A.R.T. of
GOAL SETTING

WRITTEN BY **ADAM SIA** | ILLUSTRATED BY **AH LIOW**

ASIAPAC • SINGAPORE

Publisher
ASIAPAC BOOKS PTE LTD
629 Aljunied Road
#04-06 Cititech Industrial Building
Singapore 389838
Tel: (65) 7453868
Fax: (65) 7453822
Email apacbks@singnet.com.sg

Visit us at our Internet home page
http://www.span.com.au/asiapac.htm

First published March 1997

©1997 ASIAPAC BOOKS, SINGAPORE
ISBN 981-3068-54-X

Cover design by Jonathan Yip
Body text in Comic Sans 8pt
Printed in Singapore by Chung Printing

Publisher's Note

The entire human race is fast moving towards the 21st century, an era which will bring new adjustments as well as opportunities. To be equipped for challenges in the new age, it is vital to fortify our minds with powerful and motivational thoughts. *LIVING 21 SERIES* is designed to equip modern readers with the gems of timeless principles for successful and effective living, whether at home, at work or studies.

The next millenium will also witness a fuller impact of the Asian Renaissance, as described by trend forecaster John Naisbitt in his bestselling *MEGATRENDS ASIA*. What better way to be aligned with the emergence of the East than tapping on the vast resources in Chinese culture and heritage.

We would like to thank Adam Sia and Ah Liow for the making of this unprecedented volume, and to Professor Wang Xuewen for the foreword. Our thanks, too, to the production team for putting in their best efforts to make this publication possible.

LIVING 21 SERIES
Chinese A.R.T. of Goal Setting
Chinese T.A.C.T.I.C.S. in Negotiation
Chinese Art of Leadership
Chinese Art of Excellence
Chinese Art of Team Building
Chinese Art of Commitment

About the Cartoonist

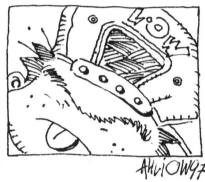

Born in Malaysia in 1966, Liow Wee Liang or Ah Liow (as he prefers to be known) studied in the Central Academy of Art in Malaysia. Upon graduation, he worked as an F.A. artist and visualizer before becoming an assistant to established comic artist Yap Ting.

During an interim period in his career, he visited various countries in Europe and worked as a street-side artist for two years.

In 1992, he returned to Malaysia where he found his niche in drawing comics. His works include features like *Agent, Wonder Bean*, and *K.L. 2000*, all published regularly in the Japanese comics *Fantasi*. Since 1994, his illustrations have been used for the cover design of *Ujang*, a popular Malay comic series.

Presently a freelance artist, he contributes regularly to comic periodicals like *Ujang 2* and Chinese lifestyle comics. He is also the cartoonist for another book in this series entitled *The Chinese Art of Excellence*.

Foreword

The 5,000-year-long civilized history of China abounds with experience related to management which has commanded increasing attention of the world. Yet its vastness and profundity coupled with the language barrier have made many people hang back . The English comic series on Chinese management published by Asiapac Books will no doubt provide an easier access to this treasure of wisdom. Practical ideas of management are offered to the reader concisely and vividly by way of illustration with lucid explanation, which provides easy and interesting reading to people of different age and educational background.

The first step for successful management as indicated in the title of the first volume of the series is goal setting which in Chinese is closely related to the will. It is interesting to note that the Chinese proverb "he who has a will is sure to succeed" (有志者事竟成) expressing the importance of the will is strikingly similar to the English one: "where there's a will there's a way". That, of course, does not mean a goal can be set beyond one's own ability and conditions. It is achievable only when based on careful assessment of one's own resources and capacity.

The ideas of goal setting are rendered more convincing with examples of famous historical figures. We cannot help admiring their dedication and perseverance, which aroused their creativity and made the seemingly impossible a possibility. Their successes achieved through well-timed proper methods and strenuous efforts are a source of inspiration, while the failures resulting from inconsistency, complacency, or indulgence in comfort and luxury are good lessons for us to learn. Yet merely philosophizing about goal setting without getting started is of no use. Let's seize the day and read the series, and in setting our goal, make the first step towards effective management.

Professor Wang Xuewen
Dean of School of International Studies
University of International Business & Economics (UIBE), Beijing

Contents

PROLOGUE

In the Chinese language, goal setting (立志) is closely associated with the will.*

Will...

All human beings have a will.

$$E = MC^2$$

*Will = 志 (zhi)

To will is to act upon a plan in one's mind.

ABRACADABRA!

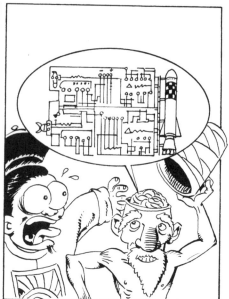

4

In doing so, we awaken the giant within each of us.

If you share the same desire, join us to savour the rich thoughts of the sages.

THE A.R.T. OF GOAL SETTING

Have you ever wondered why some people seem to be able to achieve their goals with such certainty?

While ...

... our own resolutions quickly dissipate and are too soon forgotten.

What do these people have that we don't?

Or do successful goal setters have an inborn tenacity which we don't?

The answer is a definite NO!

Although we each have a unique make-up,

we have all been given similar resources to work with.

Each of us have 168 hours to spend each week.

Most of us have average mental capacities.

We are just as capable of setting goals and achieving them as anyone else.

TARGET

We only need to keep in mind a few pointers that are really workable.

There are three components in the A.R.T. of goal setting. All goals should be ...

... Achievable ...

... Reviewed ...

... Timed.

TIME OUT FOR NOW!

Burning Passion for a Vision

Nothing in the world can be accomplished without a firm will. The mastery of every craft originates from a strong will.

Wang Yangming
(Common Traditional Teachings)

A person with a strong will must surely succeed.

Later Records of the Hans

Nothing in the world is beyond the ability of people. The only missing factor is a person of resolute mind.

Author unknown

Before one is given an awesome responsibility by heaven, his resolution is first tested, then his flesh is buffeted, his appetite repressed, his body left in want and his mental perplexity unresolved. This will produce perseverance in him and make up for his deficiencies.

Mencius
(The Book
of Mencius)

Aspiring to impact the world is the prerequisite to creating a colossal influence on the world.

Chen Liang
(Han Sayings)

Once a person makes a resolution, it must be immovable like a mountain. How can it vary and shift with the change of environment?

Yelü Chucai
(Journey to the West)

A great man is a man of many high ambitions.

Li Bai (*Journal of the Trip to Shang An Zhou*)

15

Knowing the Limits of One's Strengths

Daydreams are elusive and they encourage us to think of aims that we do not have the ability or resources to achieve. Goals, on the other hand, are made after a careful assessment of our capacity to fulfill them.

Story 1: Qi's Puny Attempts at Revolt

During the Spring and Autumn Period, the small state of Qi attacked the larger state of Chu.

With their meagre strength, Qi's soldiers were naturally defeated.

Political commentators had this to say:

Qi did not consider the limits of her own strength.

It would have been wiser that Qi form an alliance with other friendly states rather than

attack a much larger state like Chu.

Moral: Always consider one's own strengths and limitations to decide on the best strategy to achieve a goal.

Story 2: Kua Fu Chases the Sun

In Chinese mythology, it was said that during the ancient times, there lived a giant named Kua Fu.

He had extraordinary strength and could walk as fast as a flying arrow.

One day, he could not stand the heat of the sun any more.

This hateful sun! It brings the whole world such discomfort. I must teach it a lesson.

He wanted to stop the sun's insolence.

Along the way, he felt utterly parched.

Soon he was just several *li** away from the blazing ball.

Phew! This is hot. My tongue is sticking to the roof of my mouth. I must have a drink.

* 1 li is equivalent to 0.5 km.

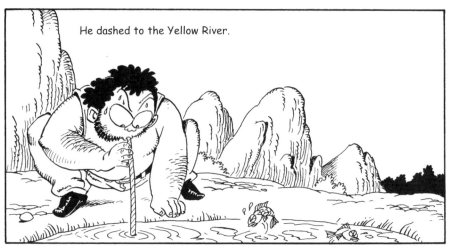

He dashed to the Yellow River.

I'm still so thirsty.
I need more water!
More ...

At the Wei River.

Even after emptying two rivers, his thirst was not quenched. Seeing the great lakes of the North, he decided to consume their contents.

Unfortunately, before he arrived at the lake...

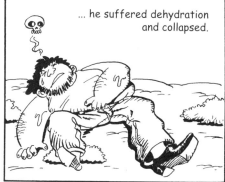

... he suffered dehydration and collapsed.

Moral: There is a heavy price to pay for not working within one's own limits.

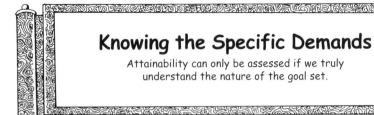

Knowing the Specific Demands

Attainability can only be assessed if we truly
understand the nature of the goal set.

Story 1: Ye Gong the Dragon Enthusiast

Ye Gong lived during the Spring and Autumn Period and cherished a liking for dragons.

This is my dragon collection.

Ye Gong fled towards the hall ...

... but was waylaid more than once.

Story 2: Go Fishing Up the Tree?!!

Once the King of Qi was chatting with Mencius.

Why does Your Majesty demand that your troops risk their lives by invading other states?

I'm not an unreasonable person. I'm merely trying to realize my dreams.

What is Your Majesty's heart desire? Does Your Majesty not have enough to wear, or is the entertainment in the palace not to your liking?

No. It's none of these.

I understand now. Your Majesty wants to be the sovereign of all under heaven! But your method is inappropriate.

The king is like a man who goes fishing ...

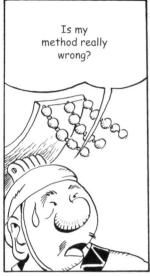

Is my method really wrong?

Yes. If you continue to oppress smaller states, an uprising against you may even take your life. Instead, you should adopt a policy of benevolent rule.

Good suggestion! I'll do just what you say.

Moral: Knowing the proper method to achieve an end is of utmost importance.

Having Determination

Determination is setting a goal and holding on until its completion. This means being mentally prepared for various obstacles along the way. For those pitfalls that we cannot envisage, our grit will help see us through.

Story 1: Break the Cooking Pot and Sink the Boat

When the Qin Dynasty was in its sunset years, there was chaos throughout the land.

The King of Qin abused his power, causing many brave men to flock to his rival—Xiang Yu of the state of Chu.

29

One day, the mighty Qin general Zhang Han proposed a campaign to conquer the state of Zhao.

This land shall be mine! All mine! Ha! Ha! Ha!

Xiang Yu got wind of the plot.

This is outrageous! We must not let Zhang Han and the tyrant King of Qin have their way.

O King! If Qin conquers Zhao, it will be a threat to us. We must assist Zhao in resisting Qin.

King Huai

I disagree! We should let Zhao exhaust the Qin army first, then our victory would be sure.

Song Yi

Very good, Song Yi. You shall be in charge of this expedition. Take all you need.

Xiang Yu deliberated on the matter and arrived at a conclusion about Song Yi.

Song Yi is a traitor!!! The weak state of Zhao will surely be defeated and then Qin will use its resources against us.

Die, you traitor! For 46 days, you merely made our troops wait like sheep to be slaughtered.

The treacherous Song Yi was plotting against our state. I was sent to kill him.

31

LONG LIVE THE KING! WELL DONE, XIANG YU!

Xiang Yu is a harsh man. We must follow his instructions or face severe punishment.

Your Majesty! Song Yi is a traitor and I've eliminated him.

Good job, Xiang Yu. I appoint you Commander in Chief.

General Xiang Yu, we've failed to penetrate the defences of Ju Lu. Please give us your assistance.

I'll bring all my men to help you.

32

Xiang Yu led his entire army across the river.

Our soldiers are not putting in enough effort. I must make them fight till their last breath.

Do or die, you must complete this mission in three days. Sink all the boats and smash all the cooking pots. We will rather die than return in shame without victory!

Moral: After nine ferocious battles, the Qin army was defeated. Xiang Yu showed his determination by destroying all avenues of retreat. If we make ourselves pay a high price when we fail, we will certainly do our best.

Story 2: Geng Yan the Undaunted Warrior

Geng Yan lived during the Eastern Han Period.

I want to be a soldier when I grow up.

Geng Yan joined Liu Xiu's command when he came of age and quickly rose to the rank of general.

Once, Liu Xiu sent Geng Yan to subdue Zhang Bu in the Dong Qing province.

34

Soon Geng Yan captured three cities in the province, including the city of Lin Zi. This unnerved Zhang Bu.

Taking up command himself, Zhang Bu counterattacked to claim Lin Zi back.

In the midst of chaos, Geng Yan was shot.

Being a man of great courage, he refused to give up.

Gritting his teeth, he continued to battle.

This letter says that Geng Yan is wounded in his thigh but continues to lead in the battle. We must send him some support.

General! Since reinforcements are on the way, and we're losing ground, why don't we retreat and wait?

We mustn't pass the buck to someone else, especially when the situation is so adverse.

Geng Yan mustered all the strength he had, attacked Zhang Bu and eventually emerged the winner.

Geng Yan. In the past I was too afraid to subdue Zhang Bu. But now I know when there's a will, there's a way.

Moral: The battle is lost when our determination wanes in the face of difficulty.

Story 3: The Secret of Tai Dou's Superb Driving Skill

Zao Fu, who lived during the Spring and Autumn Period, was under the tutelage of master driver Tai Dou.

For three long years, he was made to do menial work.

Zao Fu did his chores although they seemed pointless.
One day...

COME WITH ME!

Zao Fu tried to follow suit.

To walk on the stumps, you must use more than your feet.

After three days of nonstop practice...

Well done, Zao Fu! It takes the same dedication to master driving!

In the end, Zao Fu became a renowned cavalry man, just like his master.

Moral: If we are dedicated to the goals we have set, we will surely give our full concentration to the task at hand.

Creativity in Problem Solving

When you are beset with difficulties, and there seems to be no way out, put on your thinking cap. Check out all other possibilities—a solution may well avail itself.

Story 1: Lu Wenshu Splits the Reeds

During the Western Han Period, there was a poor shepherd boy named Lu Wenshu.

He longed for the chance to learn reading and writing.

Records of the Historian

Determined to pursue his goal, he borrowed all the books he could lay his hands on.

Just lend it to me for a few days.

He so enjoyed reading the classic *Records of the Historian* that he wanted a copy for himself.

I know! I'll make a copy of the classic for myself.

Suddenly, an idea struck him.

These reeds will make a good mat if I weave them together. I can then use them to make a scroll.

43

From then on, Wenshu began weaving mats.

He copied many books onto them.

When Wenshu grew up, he was enlisted by the king's court because of his knowledge.

No matter how little our resources may be, creative use of them can significantly improve our chances of success.

Story 2: Gong Yanghong Shaves Bamboo

During the Han Period, there lived a rich man who owned a vast library.

Unfortunately, his children showed no interest in their studies.

What's the use of having so many books without having anyone to read them?

Unknown to the rich man, he had a poor servant named Gong Yanghong who yearned to study.

May I borrow one of your books, master?

All right. I'll lend you the Spring-Autumn Annals for five days. But if you damage the book, I'll deduct a year's wages from you.

Thank you, master.

Yanghong spent all his leisure hours on the book.

Such a good book. But pity, I've to return it in five days. Sigh!

He gathered some bamboo strips and had them shaven. These he strung into a scroll.

Then he copied every word of the annals into it.

You may have free access to my library since you like studying so much.

From that day onwards, Yanghong spent hours reading and writing.

Later he was talent-spotted by the imperial palace and became a high-ranking official.

Determination and earnestness naturally arouse creativity in us.

Story 3: Che Yin and the Firefly Lamp

At a young age, Che Yin, who lived during the Eastern Jin Dynasty, was a keen learner, often reading late into the night.

One evening...

MOTHER! THE LAMP IS OUT.

OH DEAR! WE'VE RUN OUT OF LAMP FUEL.

Then I can't read in the evening any more.

Che Yin did not have to worry about buying lamp fuel any more. For the whole summer, he studied under firefly lamps.

With creativity, we can make up for all disadvantages.

REVIEWED

Regulate yourself to focus on the goal.

Keeping Distractions Away

Count the cost of your endeavours before you begin.
We must be willing to sacrifice time, money or our
desires to strive towards our target.

Story 1: Sun Jing Keeps the Doors Locked

Sun Jing, who lived during the Western Han Period, loved reading so much that he often locked himself in the house for days on end.

Come out, Sun Jing! Let's have some fun!

Yeah, we'll have a rolling good time!

He often read late into the night.

Wake up, dear! You're drooling all over your books.

Come to bed, darling ... X...XXX

I'd rather spend the evening with my books.

56

With his dedication, Sun Jing produced many fine literary works.

His fame spread far and wide, making him a renowned scholar of the period.

Moral: Sun Jing took great pains to overcome all obstacles that stood between him and his goal. His determination made him dismiss all distractions, even his biological needs.

Story 2: Su Qin Pierces His Thigh

Su Qin, who lived during the Warring States Period, studied military strategy.

MILITARY SCHOOL

When he had completed his training,

he offered his services to the King of Qin.

Not qualified.

DIPLO

When he got home, his wife gave him the cold shoulder.

HONEY ! I'M HOME!!

I'm starving, dear! Please cook me something.

GO COOK IT YOURSELF! YOU USELESS OAF!

Dad! Mom! I'm back.

I've put so much hope on him.

What a sorry sight!

He knew that they treated him badly because of the King's rejection.

I KNOW I'M NOT A FAILURE! I'LL SHOW THEM!

He made up his mind to discover the secrets behind military strategy.

Day quickly turned to night and Su Qin's eyelids weighed heavier and heavier.

How can I be sleeping now?

THIS SHOULD KEEP ME AWAKE!

The stunts in this story are performed under special circumstances. Children, don't ever attempt!

60

After one year of hard work, Su Qin sought an audience with the King once again.

SUPERB ANSWER! WELL DONE! BRAVO!

Su Qin won the King's praises with the insightful answers learnt through his diligence.

We must be willing to pay the price for success. For Su Qin, it is taking the drastic action of piercing himself.

Story 3: Da Yu Controls the Floods

A long time ago the rivers spilled over and flooded the lands.

A man named Gun led everyone to safety.

Construct channels here, here and here to drain the water out to the sea.

The project took so long to complete that Gun and his generation did not see the fruits of their labour.

After Gun's death, his son Da Yu took over his father's place.

Is that Daddy?!

I think so.

Due to his dedication, Da Yu passed his home a few times, but did not enter it.

After a few years, the work force was due to pass his hometown again.

Why don't you visit your family? Go see how your children have grown.

Isn't everyone here in the same plight?

When we have tamed the floods, we will all return to our homes together.

If we press on, we will soon complete the project.

Da Yu's team finally completed the project and all the men returned home to be reunited with their family.

Da Yu refused to allow his family become a distraction. How many distracting activities are we willing to forgo to work towards our goal?

The Problem of Complacency

Those who are complacent get caught in a rut and indulge in self-satisfaction. They do not realize that their inactivity robs them of the chance to attain their full potential, to mature and to learn.

Story 1: Chong Er Loses Sight of His Goal

The state of Jin of the Spring and Autumn Period was in great peril.

I have let my ancestors down. The empire my forefathers left me with is gone.

I may be a refugee now but I'll be back to claim my throne!

Meanwhile, the Duke of Qi made Chong Er his son-in-law, expecting him to return to power.

I betroth my daughter Jiang to you. Take good care of her.

I'll not disappoint you.

Seven years passed quickly.

Yes. That's worrying.

But what can we do?

My nephew Chong Er seems to have forgotten his ambition.

66

Jiang your husband is too contented with life here. He's forgotten about his throne!

You really feel so?

Chong Er has become too contented. That's the main problem.

Dear, I know of your ambition to become the King of Jin. Staying here is no help!

I think you're mistaken.

Go, my husband. Your will has weakened because you needn't work for anything here.

A simple lifestyle is good enough for me. I don't want to be king any more.

67

What can we do now, Uncle Zi Fan? Chong Er refuses to go!

Hmm... I know! We'll intoxicate him with wine and then bring him back to Jin.

Zi Fan and Jiang carried out their plan.

When he was drunk....

After a few years, Chong Er succeeded in becoming King of Jin.

We become slothful and weak-willed when we immerse ourselves in too much luxury.

Story 2: Gou Jian Remembers His Humiliation

During the Spring and Autumn Period, the state of Wu fought the state of Yue for the region of Jiang Nan.

Seeing the advances Wu is making, Gou Jian became nervous.

Your Majesty! We are surrounded and we have only 5,000 men left.

To conserve our strength, we must seek a diplomatic resolution. Send an envoy!

I'll stop the war on one condition. Gou Jian must be my slave.

Gou Jian accepted the condition.

HA! HA! HA! HA! HA!

It's been three years, I've had enough of you. You may go, but...

WATCH YOUR STEPS OR ELSE!

I will, Your Majesty.

In order to keep his resolve to have his revenge, Gou Jian refused all material comforts.

Please have a rest. You have been ploughing the field for a long time.

NO!

71

Please lay this quilt on the straw, sir.

No. I want to remember the humiliation and hard times as a slave.

After ten years, the state of Yue defeated the state of Wu and King Fu Cha took his own life. The state of Yue eventually became the strongest of all the states during that time.

When a goal is set, it is important to keep our resolutions strong.

Story 3: Waiting for a Rabbit under the Tree

There was a farmer who lived during the Song Period.

While working in the field one day...

I WIN!

The farmer got a free lunch without working at it at all.

73

The next day, the farmer sat under the tree and waited for the whole day. No rabbit appeared.

Perhaps the rabbit will appear tomorrow.

Many days passed without any sign of a rabbit. The farmer's crops withered a little each day and his field soon wasted away.

It is an elusive dream to hope to gain without working hard.

Story 4: Lu Sheng and His Golden Millet Dream

During the Tang Dynasty, there lived a man named Lu Sheng who wanted to become an imperial scholar.

En route to the capital, he stopped at Han Dan and met a priest.

Greetings! I'm Lü Weng. It's an honour to meet a promising scholar.

When will a poor scholar like me ever reach a place of prominence?

Don't fret. Rest your head on this pillow. When you wake up, your dreams will come true.

Thanks!

76

Please...Please. Lead the way.

Squire Cui had high regards for the scholar.

He decided to give him his daughter's hand in marriage.

So Lu Sheng settled down at the Cui's residence.

One day...

Darling, I cannot forget my aspiration. I will set off for the capital today to win an imperial title.

My Bonnie lies over the mountains, O bring back my Bony to me...Oops Bonnie!

With flying colours, Lu Sheng passed his examinations and soon became the prime minister.

His wife gave him five sons who became great scholars.

Lu Sheng was prime minister for 10 years and lived to celebrate his 80th birthday.

At that moment, Lu Sheng was jolted awake.

Sigh! Pleasant dreams never last. I guess I'm just like the millet cooking in the pot—full of potential for good taste but not prepared by the fire of hard work.

Dreams are illusions but success is made of toil and labour.

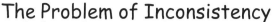

The Problem of Inconsistency

Like floating down a river, working towards a goal
requires continuous effort if we do not want to risk
being swept away by the raging torrents.

Story 1: One Hot Ten Cold

Mencius was a great teacher of morals.

Many virtuous scholars flocked to hear his wisdom.

The King of Liang also joined in as a seeker.

It comes as no surprise that the King is not wise.

WHY DO YOU SAY THAT?

Just look at any sturdy plant. Expose it to the sun for one day.

Consider the example of Mr Chiu, the great chess master, and his disciples.

One disciple concentrates on the lessons wholeheartedly.

The other allows himself to daydream and learn only part of the skill.

In the end...

Working towards a goal requires consistent effort. Fits and starts according to one's fancy will get one nowhere.

Story 2: Breaking the Warp to Teach her Son a Lesson

Mencius' mother requested Confucius' disciple Zi Si to take her son as his student.

At first Mencius put his heart to learning.

But as the days passed, his interest began to wane.

One day, when the teacher was out, Mencius and his classmates played truant.

Why are you so late today?

Sensing something amiss, Mencius' mother questioned him further.

I came from a game of hide-and-seek.

Studying is so boring.

In a fit of anger, Mencius' mother severed the warp on the loom.

Story 3: Wang Xian No Longer Thinks Too Highly Of Himself

When Wang Xian was seven, his father began teaching him calligraphy.

One day, his father decided to test his skill in writing.

Good concentration. If you practise hard, you'll become an accomplished calligrapher.

A few days later, his father went out to run some errands.

Mother, I want to go out and play.

No! You've not practised writing for two days.

Father has commended me for my writing. It's unnecessary for me to practise.

He decided to play with his friends.

89

While he was out playing, Wang Xian's father returned home and saw his unfinished character.

He picked up the pen and filled in the dot.

I'll show Mother. I'm sure she'll praise me.

When Wang Xian came back...

Mother, is my writing standard on a par with Father's?

Oh no! It is far from your father's standard. All except for this dot.

But I had forgotten to put the dot in.

91

The Problem of Discouragement

When the label of failure threatens to stick itself to us, and discouragement tails our path, ward it off with perseverance. The eventual success will prove to be even sweeter.

Story 1: The Uneasily Affected Gong Shuban

Gong Shuban was a famous craftsman of the Warring States Era. He was so good at his carving that it is difficult to tell the living from the carvings.

One night, he saw a phoenix in his dream.

When morning came...

It's so beautiful. I must reproduce it in wood for all to see.

After many rounds of work, he felt that the sculpture was complete.

He unveiled his creation to his mother and wife.

HAWK?!

I think it's a scarecrow.

I know I can sculpt a phoenix just like the one in my dream.

Not discouraged by the negative feedback, Shuban started remodelling his sculpture.

After a few days...

WHAT A MARVELLOUS PIECE!

It looks alive.

Never be discouraged when initial attempts do not produce good results. Perseverance will yield the desired outcome in due time.

Story 2: What's the Point of Looking Back?

Meng Min, who lived during the Eastern Han Period, was a straightforward person who wasted no time.

One day, he was carrying his earthen steamer to wash by the river.

Along the way...

Meng Min picked himself up.

Without batting an eyelid, he went on his way.

What a strange person! He went off without even looking at his broken steamer.

Among the crowd was a great scholar Guo Tai, who had gone into recluse.

WAIT A MINUTE, YOUNG MAN!

Why did you take off without even looking at the steamer you broke?

Would the steamer mend itself if I did? Instead of stopping to blame myself, I might as well do what I'm supposed to.

Well said! You have the makings of a scholar. I'd be your teacher if you agree.

So Meng Min became Guo Tai's student and later achieved fame as a great scholar.

Time and energy spent feeling downcast is much better used for other more productive work.

TIMED

Seize the day, lay hold of providence
and press on towards the goal.

Pacing Oneself

We should appoint a time for our goals to be accomplished—the hour, day, week, month, or the year—to help us guard against procrastination. On the other hand, it also takes patience to make our goals a reality.

Story 1: More Haste Less Speed

Zi Xia was appointed a magistrate of a neighbouring county in the state of Lu.

Before I leave for Lu, I must consult my master Confucius for tips on government administration.

Master, please give me your advice before I take up office.

Zi Xia has always been an impetuous person. He only thinks of the immediate.

Think not merely about the urgent but the end result. Focus on only the immediate will prevent you from doing great things.

Goals must be accomplished methodically. Allocate a proper amount of time for each step of the process to be completed.

Story 2: Plucking Up Courage with the First Drum

During the Spring and Autumn Period, the state of Qi invaded the state of Lu.

Cao Gui, we must personally command the troops at battle.

At the battlefield...

The Qi army beat the drums to launch an attack as soon as they saw the enemy at a distance.

The Duke of Lu wanted to retaliate by sounding their drum immediately.

Wait a moment, my lord.

The Qi drums sounded three times.

Sound the drums now, my lord.

The Lu army won the battle against Qi.

Why did you advise me to sound the drum only after the enemy has struck his drum three times?

In a battle, the men's morale is the most important. By the third beat of the drum, the enemy's courage had waned. We only sounded our drums then and thus won at the first swoop.

Enthusiasm, like courage, wanes with time. Procrastination dissipates the zest for carrying out a task. Therefore we should not take too long to achieve our goal.

Opportunity

Seize the day! It is easy to forget that time and life is
limited amidst the golden rays each sunrise floods us in.
The reality is our lifespan and opportunities are all limited.

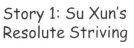

Story 1: Su Xun's Resolute Striving

Su Xun, shouldn't you be studying? Seize your chance to study when you are young.

Young Su Xun often whiled his time away, which worried his brothers.

In a twinkling of an eye, Su Xun passed his 27th birthday.

He joined a few friends for a wine-tasting session.

His friends began pitting their skills at poetry against one another.

The moonlight glimmers behind the pines...

Su Xun, why don't you complete the poem for us?

Er...the pines ... the pines...

Ha! Ha! It only shows how little you studied.

The words seared Su Xun's heart.

106

He felt ashamed of himself and resolved to increase his knowledge.

Su Xun had two young sons then. Unlike their father, Su Shi and Su Zhe were intelligent and had a great thirst for knowledge.

Pa, we want to learn to read and write.

Very good. This is a healthy desire.

After some time, father and sons were enlisted into the king's service. They came to be known as the "Three Sus".

Seize the day! It's never too early to set your goals. Do it before you become hard pressed and feel inadequate to meet the challenge.

Story 2: Time Cherishing Zhang Jiucheng

In a court tussle between loyal official Zhang Jiucheng and treacherous Qin Hui,

Jiucheng was exiled to an isolated temple.

Seizing the most of the peace and quiet the temple afforded, he began to study day and night.

Why would an old man like you bother to study so much?

There is no end to learning!
Time waits for no man.
This is my chance.

Every morning ...

Come have breakfast, dear. Quit standing at the window.

After 14 years, Minister Nan An arrived with good news.

Qin Hui has passed on. The King summons Your Honour back to the palace.

Story 3: Zhao Pu Studies Late into the Night

During the Song Dynasty, Zhao Pu was appointed secretary of the court in charge of handling all official documents. Not being well educated, he made many mistakes in the course of his duties.

I WANT THE TRADE AGREEMENT, NOT THE WESTERN GATE AGREEMENT!

I deserve to die, Your Majesty! My vocabulary is just too limited.

But as secretary of the court, you should be well read. You must make every effort to improve yourself.

So Zhao Pu worked as a secretary in the day and studied at night.

"Do not blame your fortune or others. From the ordinary we learn the profound..." Such wisdom!

One day, when Zhao Pu was absorbed in his books ...

The Emperor is here, master.

Then you've really understood the essence of *The Analects*.

After a few years, the heir apparent ascended the throne. He commended Zhao Pu for his discernment and efficiency.

We are never too old to learn. Neither are we too old to set goals and work towards them.

Perseverance

More often than not, we do not achieve our goals at the first attempt. Unless we decide to grit our teeth and press on, our aspirations will remain a figment of our imagination.

Story 1: Grinding a Rod into a Needle

Li Bai, the famous Tang poet, often played truant when he was young.

While loitering in the streets one day, he spotted an old woman rubbing a metal rod against a grinding slab.

She's right! With perseverance we can accomplish anything.

From that day onwards he never played truant again but pored over his books daily.

Perseverance will make the seemingly impossible become a possibility.

Story 2: The Foolish Old Man who Moved the Mountain

On the Northern Mountains, there lived Foolish Old Man and his family.

I'm almost 90. At my age, there is nothing much left for me to do.

But...

One thing has irked me over the years.

One day, he could tolerate it no longer, so he gathered his family.

Let's work together to remove those loathsome mountains!

GREAT IDEA!

YES! LET'S DO IT

We'll deal with it once and for all.

Shh! You can hardly level a mound. Where can you move the mountain to?

We can move the earth and rocks to the Bohai Sea.

The next day, the Wise Old Man saw the Foolish Old Man and his crew toiling away.

Ha! Ha! Hee! Hee! You're really dumb. At your age you can hardly pluck the grass. How can you level a mountain?

I'm not as silly as you think. I may not live very much longer, but my descendants will multiply. The mountain cannot grow any bigger but my workforce will.

Slowly but surely, the old man and his family chipped the mountain away bit by bit. Several generations later, his descendants succeeded in removing the mountains.

With perseverance, even the most difficult task can be tackled, the greatest challenge met, and the tallest mountain moved.

Story 3: Jingwei Fills Up the Sea

During the ancient times, the daughter of Emperor Yandi was playing on the beach of the Eastern Sea.

HELP! HELP!

After her death, her spirit became a little bird.

All day long, the bird could be heard crying.

JINGWEI! JINGWEI!

Nicknamed the Jingwei bird, it picked twigs and pebbles from the Western Hills and dropped them into the sea every day.

Year after year, she never stopped working to fill up the sea. Eventually she died when the abrasive twigs and pebbles she carried wore out her beak.

The spirit of Jingwei is exemplary because it never gave up.

CONCLUSION

Strategy & Leadership Series by Wang Xuanming

Thirty-six Stratagems: Secret Art of War
Translated by Koh Kok Kiang (cartoons) &
Liu Yi (text of the stratagems)
A Chinese military classic which emphasizes deceptive schemes to achieve military objectives. It has attracted the attention of military authorities and general readers alike.

Six Strategies for War: The Practice of Effective Leadership
Translated by Alan Chong
A powerful book for rulers, administrators and leaders, it covers critical areas in management and warfare including: how to recruit talents and manage the state; how to beat the enemy and build an empire; how to lead wisely; and how to manoeuvre brilliantly.

Gems of Chinese Wisdom: Mastering the Art of Leadership
Translated by Leong Weng Kam
Wise up with this delightful collection of tales and anecdotes on the wisdom of great men and women in Chinese history, including Confucius, Meng Changjun and Gou Jian.

Three Strategies of Huang Shi Gong: The Art of Government
Translated by Alan Chong
Reputedly one of man's oldest monograph on military strategy, it unmasks the secrets behind brilliant military manoeuvres, clever deployment and control of subordinates, and effective government.

100 Strategies of War: Brilliant Tactics in Action
Translated by Yeo Ai Hoon
The book captures the essence of extensive military knowledge and practice, and explores the use of psychology in warfare, the importance of building diplomatic relations with the enemy's neighbours, the use of espionage and reconnaissance, etc.

Latest Titles in
Strategy & Leadership Series

Chinese Business Strategies

The Chinese are known for being shrewd businessmen able to thrive under the toughest market conditions. The secret of their success lies in 10 time-tested principles of Chinese entrepreneurship.

This book offers readers 30 real-life, ancient case studies with comments on their application in the context of modern business.

Sixteen Strategies of Zhuge Liang

Zhuge Liang, the legendary statesman and military commander during the Three Kingdoms Period, is the epitome of wisdom.

Well-grounded in military principles of Sun Zi and other masters before him, he excelled in applying them in state administration and his own innovations, thus winning many spectacular victories with his uncanny anticipation of enemy moves.